LITERATURE

EDITED BY NICK WINNICK

Weigl

Published by Weigl Educational Publishers Limited
6325 10 Street SE
Calgary, Alberta, Canada
T2H 2Z9

Website: www.weigl.com

Library and Archives Canada Cataloguing in Publication data available upon request.
Fax 403-233-7769 for the attention of the Publishing Records department.

ISBN 978-1-55388-967-0 (hard cover)
ISBN 978-1-55388-970-0 (soft cover)

Printed in the United States of America
1 2 3 4 5 6 7 8 9 0 13 12 11 10 09

All of the Internet URLs given in the book were valid at the time of publication. However, due to the dynamic nature of the Internet, some addresses may have changed, or sites may have ceased to exist since publication. While the author and publisher regret any inconvenience this may cause readers, no responsibility for any such changes can be accepted by either the author or the publisher.

Weigl acknowledges Getty Images as its primary image supplier for this title.
Detail of British Columbia Archives: page 31 bottom.

Every reasonable effort has been made to trace ownership and to obtain permission to reprint copyright material. The publishers would be pleased to have any errors or omissions brought to their attention so that they may be corrected in subsequent printings.

We acknowledge the financial support of the Government of Canada through the Book Publishing Industry Development Program (BPIDP) for our publishing activities.

EDITOR: Nick Winnick
DESIGN: Terry Paulhus

Literature
Contents

Literature
Through The Years

Writing has been one of the most important human activities for thousands of years. People write to entertain each other, to keep records of events, and to preserve what they discover about the world and about themselves. Each place and time has its own special style of writing that tells its own story about how people think and feel.

In the early years of Canadian literature, many writers were immigrants. French, British, and other European settlers wrote about the hardships and successes of frontier life. They wrote of the landscape, natural beauty, and solitude.

In the mid-20th century, many Canadian writers were part of families that had lived in Canada for generations. They began to write about the unique Canadian experience. Life in cities was fleshed out in one enthralling book after another.

Today, Canada's literary contributors come from every part of the world and have lived in various situations. Canadian authors contribute to some of the finest literature on Earth and are known and respected around the world. Canadian writers will continue to entertain and enlighten readers long into the future.

2000s

Writer and Politician

As a journalist, historian, and statesman, Michael Ignatieff has a broad resume with a long history of achievements. He has a doctorate degree in history from Harvard and has taught at prestigious schools, such as Cambridge, Oxford, and Harvard. Ignatieff has many books and films to his credit. In 2009, as the leader of the federal Liberal Party, Ignatieff found the time to publish *True Patriot Love*, a memoir about his life and family. In *True Patriot Love*, Ignatieff follows several generations of his mother's family as they debate, publicly and privately, their ideas of what Canada is, and should be. Ignatieff explains how his grandfather returned from battle in World War I believing that Canada had earned the right to call itself an independent nation. Ignatieff's uncle, George Grant, wrote the essay "Lament for a Nation." In it, he stated his concern that Canada had become a colony, in all but name, of the United States. Ignatieff shares these perspectives, and his own, about the unique makeup of Confederation, and his vision of its future. The following passage is an excerpt from the book. "Loving a country is an act of the imagination. You love the country because it gives you the possibility of sharing feeling and belief. You cannot love the country alone. The emotions you have must be shared with others in order for them to make any sense at all. A solitary patriot is a contradiction in terms. Love of country is an emotion shared in the imagination across time, shared with the dead, the living and the yet to be born."

Writer and Politician

2001

Robert Munsch's *Love You Forever* is listed as one of the four all-time best-selling children's books by *Publishers Weekly*.

2002

Guy Vanderhaeghe publishes *The Last Crossing*.

2000s

Man for the Mountains

Sid Marty is a poet, musician, and author, but his career began very differently than that of many artists. Marty was a national park warden in the Rocky Mountains in his early years, and his experience in the mountains shaped all of his later writings. *Men for the Mountains* was the book that started a landslide of writing, and tells of the people who forged and maintained Canada's majestic western parks. *Switchbacks* picks up where *Men for the Mountains* leaves off, telling the stories of the first trailblazers in the Rockies, and the wardens who kept those paths, with a mixture of comedy, tragedy, and adventure. Marty's book, *The Black Grizzly of Whiskey Creek*, uses the story of a set of bear attacks in the 1980s to tell his larger story—how people think about, interact with, and preserve nature. Through all of Marty's writings, there is a strong advocacy of conservation. Marty reminds people, especially city-dwellers, of the importance of Canada's wild spaces and the need to preserve them.

2003	2004	2005
M.G. Vassanji's *The In-Between World of Vikram Lall* wins the Giller Prize.	Poet Nicole Markotic publishes *Widows and Orphans*.	Thomas King releases *A Short History of Indians in Canada.*

2000s

Voice of the Miramichi

A prolific writer, David Adams Richards is one of New Brunswick's favoured sons. His vibrant storytelling gives readers a deep emotional connection to the subjects of his work, which often centre around the Miramichi River. Two of Richards' best-known books, *Lines on the Water* and *Mercy Among the Children*, take place in this **quintessential** New Brunswick setting. *Mercy Among the Children* was co-winner of the Giller Prize in 2000. It tells the story of a man who vows never to express anger or violence after a childhood accident, and the consequences of living with that decision. Like much of Richards' work, *Mercy Among the Children* spans a long period of time, while Richards allows the setting and the characters to grow together and influence each other. The end result is a very realistic style of storytelling that has earned Richards much acclaim. In addition to the Giller Prize, Richards has won many other awards, including two Gemini awards for his screenwriting and the Governor General's Award in both the fiction and **nonfiction** categories. In his home province, the Writers' Federation of New Brunswick honours the best fiction book each year with the David Adams Richards Award for Fiction.

2006

Vincent Lam publishes *Bloodletting and Miraculous Cures*.

2007

Journalist Naomi Klein releases *The Shock Doctrine*, a critique of aggressive foreign policy.

Prairie Haunts

2003

Prairie Haunts

Moose Jaw's Arthur Slade has many interesting stories to tell. In high school, he began writing and found his calling. In 1997, he published his first young-adult novel, *Draugr*. This spooky story about a grandfather's chilling tales from a faraway land marked the beginning of Slade's career in the business of fright.

With titles such as *The Haunting of Drang Island*, *Ghost Hotel*, and *Monsterology* under his belt, it is clear that Slade is no stranger to the scary side of storytelling. His books have been included in such well-known series as *Northern Frights* and *Canadian Chills*. One of Slade's books, *Dust*, won the Governor General's Award for Children's Literature in 2001. *Dust* follows the story of a mysterious stranger who comes to the town of

Horshoe promising relief from a drought. When children start disappearing, teenager Robert is the only one able to see through the smoke and mirrors and the promises of prosperity to discover the stranger's secrets.

Into the Future

In 2007, more than 3,000 new books were being published every day around the world. People today have access to more information than at any other time in history. How do you think this flood of books will affect literature in the future? How will you be able to find the books you want to read among so many others?

2008

Poet and novelist Fred Wah publishes *Sentenced to Light*.

2009

Terry Glavin wins the Lieutenant Governor's Award for Literary Excellence.

Literature
1990s

The Vinyl Cafe

The show features musical guests and letters from listeners, but the centrepiece of *The Vinyl Cafe* is a weekly story about a married couple named Dave and Morley. Listeners have grown to love these characters, and McLean's distinctive storytelling style. As of 2009, McLean had published five books and six spoken albums worth of *Vinyl Cafe* stories. CBC listeners continue to be delighted by the stories of Dave and Morley, and of their fellow Canadians, every Sunday.

1992

Canada and Quebec

Quebec politicians and newspapers were in an uproar in 1992. The cause? Mordecai Richler's new book, *Oh Canada! Oh Quebec! Requiem for a Divided Country*. Richler was no stranger to controversy. His books and articles often provoked people. *Oh Canada! Oh Quebec!* was no different. It criticized Quebec separatists and accused them of being **prejudiced** against Jewish people. The separatists were not the only people criticized. Richler wrote that people in the rest of Canada were prejudiced as well. His book also questioned why Canada was always on the brink of breaking up. In *Oh Canada! Oh Quebec!*, Richler asked why the French and English could not "learn to celebrate what binds them together."

1994

The Vinyl Cafe

In 1994, short stories began to grow in popularity all across Canada. This was thanks in part to the writing of Stuart McLean.

McLean began broadcasting his short stories to Canadians as the host of a temporary summer program on the CBC called *The Vinyl Cafe*. By 1997, *The Vinyl Cafe* had become so popular that it was broadcast every Sunday.

1991
Guy Gavriel Kay's fantasy novel *Tigana* wins the Aurora Award.

1992
Todd McFarlane begins releasing *Spawn* comic books.

1993
Thomas King publishes *Green Grass, Running Water*.

Canada and Quebec

True Crime

1996

True Crime

Author Margaret Atwood did not disappoint her fans with her 1996 release, *Alias Grace*. The novel is based on a true story of murder and scandal. In 1843, 16-year-old Grace Marks was accused of murdering her employer and his housekeeper. Atwood's book tells her own version of Grace's story.

Governor General's Award Winners for Children's Literature

1990	*Redwork* by Michael Bedard
	La Vrai Histoire du chien de Clara Vic by Christiane Duchesne
1991	*Pick-Up Sticks* by Sarah Ellis
	Deux heures et demie avant Jasmine by François Gravel
1992	*Hero of Lesser Causes* by Julie Johnston
	Victor by Christiane Duchesne
1993	*Some of the Kinder Planets* by Tim Wynne-Jones
	La Route de Chlifa by Michelle Marineau
1994	*Adam and Eve and Pinch-Me* by Julie Johnston
	Une belle journée pour mourir by Suzanne Martel
1995	*The Maestro* by Tim Wynne-Jones
	Comme une peau de chagrin by Sonia Sarfati
1996	*Ghost Train* by Paul Yee
	Noémie-Le Secret de Madame Lumbago by Gilles Tibo
1997	*Awake and Dreaming* by Kit Pearson
	Pien by Michel Noël
1998	*The Hollow Tree* by Janet Lunn *Variations sur un mˆeme &*
	Lagno, T'aime by Angèle Delaunois

1994

Douglas Coupland publishes *Life After God.*

1995

bill bissett releases *Th influenza uv logik.*

The English Patient

1992

The English Patient

"*The English Patient* began with a vision: a burning man in the desert," said author Michael Ondaatje. The novel tells the story of a Canadian nurse in World War II who is caring for a dying patient in Italy. The patient tells a love story that captivates the nurse. Most of *The English Patient*'s readers were also captivated. The book won the 1992 Governor General's Award for fiction and shared the Booker Prize in Britain. It was the first time a Canadian had won the important British award. The novel was later made into an Academy Award-winning film.

1993

The Stone Diaries

Carol Shields faced more bad reviews than good reviews in her early career. When she began her master's degree at the University of Ottawa in 1965, she was one of the few married women with children in the program. The university had not wanted her to join the course, but they finally allowed her to begin. Years later, reviews of her first books were not promising. A reviewer in *Maclean's* magazine called Shields' first novel "smaller than life." As Shields continued to publish, however, more people praised her work. Then, in 1993, when she published *The Stone Diaries*, the praise would not stop. *The Stone Diaries* tells the story of a woman's life over 80 years. Among other honours, the book won a Governor General's Award in Canada and the Pulitzer Prize in the United States. At almost 60 years of age, Carol Shields had become an international publishing success.

The Stone Diaries

1996

Mordecai Richler publishes *A Year in Jerusalem*.

1997

J.D. Frazer creates *User Friendly*, one of the first major online comic strips.

1998

Tomson Highway writes *Kiss of the Fur Queen*.

The Love of Alice Munro

Writer Alice Munro has often received praise for her writing. During the last three decades she wrote short story collections, articles, and a novel. She was short-listed for the Booker Prize, and she has come away with one of Canada's highest literary awards, the Governor General's Award for Fiction, three times. Munro also won the Canadian Booksellers Association International Book Year Award and the PEN/Malamud Award for Excellence in Short Fiction, among others. In 1998, she added to that list by winning the Giller Prize for literature for her collection of short stories entitled *The Love of a Good Woman*. This book explores what people will do, both good and bad, for love.

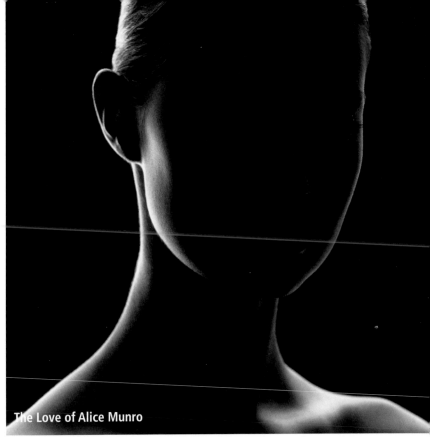

The Love of Alice Munro

Into the Future

Many movies are made from books. While movies are often better at providing description, they cannot be as complex or complete as books. Many authors have written in the hopes that their books will be chosen to be made into movies. How do you think this trend might affect literature in the future?

1999

Jan Zwicky's *Songs for Relinquishing the Earth* wins the Governor General's Award for Poetry.

2000

Newspaper tycoon Conrad Black sells most of his newspapers to media company CanWest.

Storyteller Extraordinaire

Children's publishing grew in Canada during the 1980s. One notable reason for this was children's author and storyteller Robert Munsch. Munsch was born in the United States, but he became a Canadian after he and his wife moved to Canada during the 1970s. Munsch always loved to tell stories. He decided to try writing his stories down on paper. In 1979, a Canadian publisher, Annick Press, agreed to publish Munch's first book, *Mud Puddle*. The next year, *The Paper Bag Princess* was published. This popular story about a girl who outsmarts a dragon to save her prince was an instant hit. Munsch wrote many other children's books, including *Murmel, Murmel, Murmel* and *Thomas' Snowsuit*. His books have sold millions of copies around the world.

Storyteller Extraordinaire

1981
Humorist Gary Lauten wins the Stephen Leacock Award for *Take My Family...Please!*

1982
Emile Nelligan's complete poems are released in English, translated by Fred Cogswell.

1985

Robertson Davies

Robertson Davies was one of the best-known Canadian writers for decades. Davies began his career as an actor. He was also a teacher. Davies wrote many novels, plays, and nonfiction books. In 1985, three of his most popular books were published in one volume called *The Deptford Trilogy*. In 1986, his book *What's Bred in the Bone* won the Canadian Authors' Association Literary Award for fiction. The book was also nominated for Britain's prestigious Booker Prize. *What's Bred in the Bone* was the second book of three called the Cornish series.

1986

A Turtle Named Franklin

Many Canadian children's books written during the 1980s became popular around the world. In 1986, *Franklin in the Dark* was published. This picture book featured a young turtle who was so afraid of the dark that he hated being in his shell. The book was written by Paulette Bourgeois and illustrated by Brenda Clark. Bourgeois decided to write a children's book when her daughter, Natalie, was one month old. Franklin was such a popular character that Bourgeois and Clark created many other books about him. *Hurry Up, Franklin* was published in 1989.

Robertson Davies

A Turtle Named Franklin

1983
Irving Abella releases *None is Too Many*.

1984
William Gibson releases *Neuromancer*, which inspired movies such as *The Matrix*.

1985
Mordecai Richler's *Joshua Then and Now* is made into a movie.

15

W.P. Kinsella

1980s

W.P. Kinsella

Although W.P. (Bill) Kinsella did not publish his first stories until he was 42 years old, he is one of Canada's greatest authors. Kinsella wrote short stories, novels, and articles. He first became known for a group of short stories he wrote about a character named Silas, a Cree man. In 1982, he published his most popular novel, *Shoeless Joe*. It is about a man, Ray, who is driven to mow down his cornfield to make a baseball field, where the spirits of the 1919 Chicago White Sox baseball team come to play. Although Kinsella is Canadian, many people in the United States think *Shoeless Joe* is the best novel written about America's favourite pastime. In 1989, *Shoeless Joe* was made into a major Hollywood film, *Field of Dreams*, starring Kevin Costner. Kinsella wrote several collections of short stories during the 1980s. He also wrote another popular novel about baseball, *The Iowa Baseball Confederacy*.

1985

Page and Screen

Poet and novelist Margaret Atwood wrote many popular novels over the decades. One of her best-known books, *The Handmaid's Tale*, was written in 1985. It won several awards and was made into a Hollywood film. The novel is a work of science fiction that contains a world in which women have few rights.

Page and Screen

1986
Journalist, cartoonist, and writer Ben Wicks is inducted to the Order of Canada.

1987
Jacob Two-Two and the Dinosaur is published.

1988
Longtime political cartoonist Len Norris retires from the *Vancouver Sun*.

Writing About Canada

1980s

Writing About Canada

Pierre Berton writes nonfiction books about Canada. His history books are not dry and dull, but are always full of interesting stories. During the 1980s, Berton wrote *The Klondike Quest*, which was about the search for gold in the Canadian North. *The Promised Land* explained the settlement of the West in the early part of the century. *Vimy* told about Canadians during World War I. *The Arctic Grail* was a popular book about the exploration of Canada. In 1989, Berton published *Starting Out, 1920–1947*, which was the first volume of his **autobiography**.

Into the Future

Of all the stories people read, sometimes the most memorable are those they recall from childhood. Is there a storybook that you remember reading when you were younger? What do you remember about it? Do you think that it had an effect on your imagination?

1989
The first complete collection of E.J. Pratt's poems is published.

1990
W.O. Mitchell publishes *Roses Are Difficult Here.*

1970s

The First Lady of Manawaka

Margaret Laurence began writing stories at the age of seven. She published her first fictional piece in 1954. Laurence became a Companion to the Order of Canada in 1971, was awarded the Molson Prize in 1975, and the Governor General's Award for her 1974 book, *The Diviners*. The book imitates Laurence's own experiences—it is about a woman from Manawaka. This fictional Canadian town is very much like Neepawa, Manitoba, where Laurence grew up. The main character, Morag, is also an author. Laurence wrote four books featuring Manawaka characters. These Canadian novels are considered Laurence's best. They show life in small, prairie towns. *The Diviners* was the most popular of these four Canadian novels. It is considered one of Laurence's finest novels. She also had great success with a series of books based on her experiences in Africa in the late 1960s. This celebrated author's work has been made into television, stage, and radio adaptations. The National Film Board produced a documentary about her life in 1979 called *Margaret Laurence, First Lady of Manawaka*.

The First Lady of Manawaka

1971
Margaret Atwood publishes

1972
Marshall McLuhan publishes his work

1973
Poet Paulette Jiles publishes her

Timothy Findley

Far-out Author

Monica Hughes is out of this world! Her science-fiction books have been read by young people for decades. She has written more than 30 books, such as the popular 1970s *Isis* trilogy, which included *The* *Tomorrow City*, written in 1978. Because of the success of *The Tomorrow City* and other works, Hughes has won almost every major Canadian award for young people's fiction. Her achievements have brought her popularity and readership throughout North America and Europe.

Far-out Author

1970s

Timothy Findley

Timothy Findley's 1977 novel *The Wars*, was enough to make him famous. This book, his third, gained him recognition and readers throughout the world. *The Wars* was translated into French, Dutch, Norwegian, and Spanish. It was also made into a movie in 1983, and Findley wrote the screenplay. This book earned Findley a Governor General's award, a top literary award in Canada, and it has become the most-often taught and written about of his books.

1974
Ralph Gustafson's *Fire on Stone* wins the Governor General's Award for Poetry.

1975
French-Canadian author Gabrielle Roy publishes *Un jardin au bout du monde.*

1971

Jacob Two-Two is a Huge Hit-Hit

Mordecai Richler introduced Canadian children to Jacob Two-Two in 1975. *Jacob Two-Two* *Meets the Hooded Fang* became a must-read for young people. It addressed a youngest child's feeling of being less important than his older siblings. Jacob is a six-year-old boy who repeats everything he says because he does not think people hear him the first time. He has a dream that he is taken to children's prison, where he faces the dreaded and feared head jailer, the Hooded Fang. Richler's book became one of the most popular children's books ever.

Jacob Two-Two is a Huge Hit-Hit

1972

French Success

A leading New Brunswick writer, Antonine Maillet, made a name for herself in the 1970s. Her 1979 novel called *Pelagie-la-Charrette* was a story set in the 1750s about French settlers from Nova Scotia who were forced to leave by the British. Maillet's novel followed a small group of Acadians on their return. Her writing brought her success, and she is the only writer not from France to win the French Prix Goncourt. *Pelagie-la-Charrette* became a bestseller and was translated into English in 1982.

French Success

1976

Hugh Hood releases *Dark Glasses*

1977

Robert Kroetsch revitalizes the long poem form with his work *Seed Catalogue*

1978

Lynn Johnston begins writing the comic strip *For Better or Worse*

The Life of Alice Munro

form but not in fact," and that it truly was a work of fiction. People outside Wigham loved Munro's work, and it won the Canadian Booksellers Association International Book Year Award. Alice Munro's third book of the decade, *Who Do You Think You Are?*, won her the Governor General's Award and a nomination for Britain's Booker Prize. This book of short stories was released in the United States and England under different titles. She made several last-minute changes to the collection. She changed three stories so all of the separate stories would be linked by a common character. She also wrote a new story to replace ones she had removed. The changes paid off for Munro, and her book received rave reviews and sold very well.

1970s

The Life of Alice Munro

The 1971 novel *Lives of Girls and Women* won Alice Munro attention and fame, but not everyone loved the author's work. Her home town of Wigham, Ontario, was insulted and angry when the book hit the stores. The people of Wigham thought that Munro had based her characters on citizens in the town, and some did not like how they were depicted. Munro insisted that the book was, "autobiographical in

Into the Future

Even using fiction, authors are able to speak about reality. Novels set in Canadian towns, cities, and rural areas can preserve the feelings of living in those places at one point in history. Novels can become ways to experience the past. Think about the Canadian books you have read. Can you think of any that might help future people understand how you think and how you feel right now?

1979

Novelist Roch Carrier publishes *Les enfants du bonhomme dans la lune.*

1980

Young adult author Gordon Korman publishes *Who is Bugs Potter?*

Literature
1960s

1960s

Both Sides of the Story

Two acclaimed writers gave opposite views of Quebec during the 1960s. Marie-Claire Blais wrote her first novel when she was 19. Translated into English as *Mad Shadows*, it was a grim, powerful book, loosely based on her own life. Her family was poor, and her convent school was strict. Her novel *A Season in the Life of Emmanuel*, often regarded as her best, won many prizes and made her internationally famous. Roch Carrier, on the other hand, set his best-known novel, *La guerre, yes sir!*, in a Quebec village at the beginning of the Second World War. He gave readers a warm picture of the people and customs of rural Quebec. The novel was so popular that it was adapted to the stage and performed in both French and English. Carrier wrote two more novels in the series.

1961

Writers Become Publishers

In the mid-1960s, many young writers set up their own publishing companies. They were tired of being rejected by the established firms. One such publishing company was House of Anansi, founded by Dave Godfrey and Dennis Lee in 1967. It was run from the house in which Godfrey and his wife lived. Godfrey had just returned from a year in Africa, and he named the company after a spider god in an African legend. The editors were all strong nationalists caught up in the spirit of Centennial Year, and they published fiction, poetry, literary criticism, and translations of Quebec writers. At first, they worked in a basement office, but soon the manuscripts and boxes of books overflowed onto the stairs and up to the third-floor attic. Some of the writers also lived in the house at times. Such famous writers as Margaret Atwood, Roch Carrier, and Michael Ondaatje were first published by House of Anansi.

Writers Become Publishers

1961
T.A. Goudge's *The Ascent of Life* wins the Governor General's Award for Nonfiction.

1962
The Stephen Leacock Award is given to W.O. Mitchell for *Jake and the Kid*.

1963
Farley Mowat publishes *Never Cry Wolf*.

Inuit Culture Inspires Author

James Houston was born in Toronto, Ontario, in 1921. He was an author, artist, and filmmaker. Houston greatly helped to popularize Inuit art and stories. Trained as an artist, Houston went to the Arctic as an administrator. He arrived in Inukjuak in 1948 and remained in the North until 1962. During this time, Houston lived in the traditional ways of the Inuit. He used dogsleds to travel from place to place and lived in igloos. Houston was impressed by the beautiful carvings he saw in the North and realized that these images would also work well in print-making. He taught the Inuit print-making techniques he had learned in Japan. Many of these artists became famous and successful print-makers. Houston also wrote and illustrated many books for both children and adults that are set in the Arctic and on the Northwest Coast. *Tikta' liktak* and *The White Archer* tell the stories of Inuit legends. More often, he invented his own plots, but included information about Inuit customs. In many of the adventures, Inuit characters meet up with European explorers and settlers. Houston received many awards for his work. In 1992, he was named as one of the 125 most significant people in Canada's 125-year history.

Inuit Culture Inspires Author

Marshall McLuhan coins the phrase "the medium is the message" in his book *Understanding Media*.

George Grant writes *Lament for a Nation*, decrying Canada's reliance on the United States.

Movies to Books

1964

Movies to Books

Pierre Berton, a prominent journalist and television personality, added novels to his many accomplishments and became one of Canada's most popular writers. His first book, *Klondike*, was about the gold rush of 1898; his father had been one of the gold seekers. In the 1960s, Berton published *The Secret World of Og*, a children's adventure story, and *Remember Yesterday*, a book of photographs to celebrate Canada's centennial. His other books were about food, religion, and political and business leaders. He also wrote about the building of the Canadian Pacific Railway in *The National Dream* and *The Last Spike*. Berton's books were popular because they told interesting stories about people and events that Canadians wanted to remember.

1964

Poets and Songwriters

Gilles Vigneault won the Governor General's Award for Poetry in 1965. He was already well known as a **balladeer**, songwriter, and broadcaster. His writing and songs were influenced by the folk culture of the North Shore region of Quebec, where he grew up. His voice was harsh, but as he performed, his personality grabbed the audience. That same year, singer Monique Leyrac won the grand prize for Vigneault's "Mon Pays" [My Country] at the International Song Festival. The song became a kind of anthem for the Québécois. At the St. Jean-Baptiste parade in Montreal the following year, Vigneault and Leyrac were honoured with their own float. Another poet who recited his words to music was Leonard Cohen, recognized internationally and in Canada for his haunting poem "Suzanne." His voice was gruff, and he sang in a monotone, but his album "Songs from a Room" was regarded as one of the best examples of pop as poetry. Some critics say his novel *Beautiful Losers* (1966) is the finest experimental novel ever published in Canada. Cohen won the Governor General's Award in 1968, but he refused to accept it.

Poets and Songwriters

1966

Margaret Atwood releases her third poetry collection in three years.

1967

Margaret Laurence's *A Jest of God* wins the Governor General's Award for Fiction.

1965

From Journalists to Historians

In 1966, journalist James Gray published *The Winter Years*, the first of his unusual social histories of the Prairies. It was set in the Depression of the 1930s. He vividly described the drought, dust, and grasshoppers on the plains. Gray wrote about some of the unemployed in work camps, hopping on freight trains headed for Ottawa to complain. Many people say this book is one of the best histories ever written in Canada. Peter Newman, a reporter for *Maclean's* magazine, changed political biography forever in Canada when he published *Renegade in Power* (1963). The book focussed on Prime Minister John Diefenbaker and his Conservative government. Reading Newman's books, Canadians discovered that history could be fun to read.

From Journalist to Historians

Into the Future

Canada has always been made up of a wide variety of cultures and people. First Nations, French and British settlers, and many generations of immigrants from all over the world have each contributed to Canadian identity. In what way is this a source of inspiration for authors?

1968
David Suzuki wins the Kalinga Prize for the Popularization of Science.

1969
Milton Acorn, nicknamed the People's Poet, publishes *I've Tasted My Blood.*

1970
Pierre Berton publishes *The National Dream.*

Big-time Stuff

Mowat wrote one of his most popular books, *The Dog Who Wouldn't Be*. It is a story about Mutt, who had been Mowat's family pet when he was a boy in Saskatchewan. Mutt was always causing trouble. He chased cows. He chewed gum and swallowed it. He hated being washed, so he ate the soap. Mutt reappears in *Owls in the Family*, another popular story. Two other Mowat books for young people are *The Curse of the Viking Grave* and *The Black Joke*. Some of the books Mowat wrote for adults have also been enjoyed by young readers. They include *A Whale for the Killing* and *Virunga*, the story of Dian Fossey and the mountain gorillas of Central Africa.

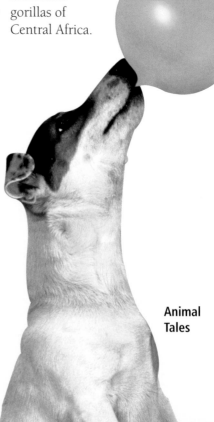

1950s

Big-time Stuff

When Morley Callaghan first began writing stories, he showed some of them to his American friend, Ernest Hemingway. Like Hemingway, he aimed to become a successful writer, and he was encouraged when Hemingway told him, "You write big-time stuff. All you have to do is keep on writing." Callaghan did keep on writing, and he eventually became famous. One reviewer called him "the most important novelist and short story writer in English Canada."

1950s

Animal Tales

"Writing books for young people has been fun," says Farley Mowat. "It has brought me—and, I hope my young readers—the feeling that life is very much worth living." Mowat's first book for young people was *Lost in the Barrens*, which won the 1956 Governor General's Award. It is an adventure story about two boys who became friends. One is Aboriginal. The other is not. When they get lost in the Barren Lands of the Arctic, they survive because of their different skills, which they share with one another. The following year,

Animal Tales

1951
Award-winning Cree playwright Tomson Highway is born in Brochet, Manitoba.

1952
E.J. Pratt publishes *Toward the Last Spike*.

1953
David Walker's *Digby* wins the Governor General's Award for Fiction.

1950s

History in Verse

Long before the luxury liner R.M.S. *Titanic* became the subject of a blockbuster movie, E.J. Pratt wrote a poem about the doomed ship. Like many of Pratt's works, *The Titanic* is an epic—a long poem that tells a story. Many of Pratt's poems celebrate events in Canadian history. *Towards the Last Spike* tells of the building of the Canadian Pacific Railway. It won Pratt his third Governor General's Award in 1952. Other Pratt poems are about his home province, Newfoundland, which he writes about with great affection. Pratt had a wonderful skill with words, brilliantly depicting a scene or idea. He has been called one of Canada's greatest poets.

History in Verse

1954

Soviet defector Igor Gouzenko publishes a novel based on his experiences.

1955

John Kricfalusi, creator of *Ren and Stimpy* and *The Ripping Friends*, is born.

1954

Hugh MacLennan Does It Again

The Watch that Ends the Night won Hugh MacLennan his fifth Governor General's Award in 1959. A story about moral courage, it has been called "the great Canadian novel." Yet MacLennan's best-known novel is probably *Two Solitudes*, about English-French relations in Canada. The term "two solitudes" has become a common phrase used to describe the relationship between English-speaking Canada and Quebec. When MacLennan published *The Watch that Ends the Night*, he was teaching English at McGill University. As a professor of English living in Quebec, MacLennan brought a unique perspective to this issue.

1959

The Governor General's Award

1959, the "Juvenile" category was dropped from the Governor General's Literary Awards. Consequently, there were only nine winners in the 1950s.

Governor General's Award Winners	
1950	*The Great Adventure* by Donalda Dickie
1951	*A Land Divided* by John F. Hayes
1952	*Cargoes on the Great Lakes* by Marie McPhedran
1953	*Rebels Ride at Night* by John F. Hayes
1954	*The Nor'westers* by Marjorie Wilkins Campbell
1955	*The Map-maker* by Kerry Wood
1956	*Lost in the Barrens* by Farley Mowat
1957	*The Great Chief* by Kerry Wood
1958	*Nikwala* by Edith L. Sharp

Hugh MacLennan Does It Again

1956
Harold Innis releases *Essays in Canadian Economic History*.

1957
The Canada Council for the Arts is formed.

1958
Acadian poet and author Antonine Maillet publishes her first novel, *Pointe-aux-Coques*.

1954

Anne Hébert

Quebec poet Anne Hébert wrote her first collection of poems in 1942. She then wrote scripts for the National Film Board and broadcasts for Radio-Canada in 1954. She released her first novel in 1958. By the time it was translated into English as *The Silent Rooms*, she had written her best-known novel, *Kamouraska*. This story, which is based on a murder in 19th-century Quebec, was made into a popular film. It also earned her France's Prix des Libraires award. While continuing to write novels, Hébert also enhanced her reputation as a poet, winning many prizes in both Canada and France. Younger poets have been greatly influenced by her style of writing.

Anne Hébert

Into the Future

The 1950s were comparatively calm after the turbulence of World War II. Writers found time to explore new ideas and new styles. Some were critical of literary traditions, while others held strongly to them. How important do you think tradition is in writing? If all writing is a combination of old and new ideas, how much of each do you think makes up a good story?

1959

Gordon R. Dickson publishes the first novel in his *Dorsai* series.

1960

Frank Underhill earns the Governor General's Award for his work *In Search of Canadian Liberalism*.

Gabriel Roy

1947

Gabriel Roy

Gabrielle Roy was born in Manitoba but settled in Montreal when the war started. There, she began working as a freelance journalist and writing her novel *Bonheur d'occasion*. It is a story about Montreal's poor at the end of the Depression. She published the novel in 1945. Roy became the first Canadian to win the Prix Fémina in Paris. She went on to win the Literary Guild of America Award in New York as well as the first of three Governor General's Awards in 1947. Her highly regarded novel was translated into 15 languages. The English version was called *The Tin Flute*. Gabrielle Roy became the first woman to become a member of the Royal Society of Canada when she was given the Lorne Pierce Medal. She continued writing novels, essays, and children's stories. She earned many awards and prizes, including the Prix Duvernay and the Molson Prize. Gabrielle Roy was also named a Companion to the Order of Canada in 1967.

1941

Poet and author Gwendolyn MacEwen is born.

1942

Poet and critic John Sutherland creates *First Statement*, a literary magazine.

Under the Volcano

Many people argue that Malcolm Lowry's *Under the Volcano* is one of the best novels in modern literature. Although not born in Canada, Lowry spent much of his time in British Columbia. Much of his fiction is set in that province, and most was at least a little autobiographical. *Under the Volcano* is no exception. He based the book on his experiences in Mexico. The novel was the product of ten years of writing and rewriting. He applied the finishing touches on Christmas Eve, 1944, but it took years before the public would read it. *Under the Volcano* was accepted for publication in 1946 and was finally published in 1947. He wrote other novels, including *Lunar Caustic*. His final novel, *October Ferry*, was published in 1970, long after his death.

Under the Volcano

1941

Emily Carr

Emily Carr spent her life being creative. She painted the Aboriginal communities in British Columbia, trying to provide a record of their disappearing culture and villages. In 1927, Carr met the Group of Seven, a group of artists who often painted landscapes. They liked her painting, and her work was included in their exhibitions. This brought her recognition and respect. In 1937, Carr had a serious heart attack. Bedridden due to her ill health, Carr found a great deal of time to write. She wrote *Klee Wyck* in 1941. The title was a name the Aboriginals called her, meaning "Laughing One." The book was a collection of pieces about themes similar to her painting—Aboriginal totems, abandoned villages, and natural scenery. Her writing was immediately successful and, to her surprise, she received the Governor General's award. The appreciation for both her writing and her painting had come late in her life. She was 70 years old when *Klee Wyck* was released. It was translated into French in 1973. Many of her writings, as well as her journals, were published after she died in 1945.

Emily Carr

1943
French-Canadian novelist Yves Beauchemin is born.

1944
Stephen Leacock passes away.

1945
Soviet agent-turned-writer Igor Gouzenko defects to Canada.

31

1945

Writing What He Knows

At first, Hugh MacLennan tried to write novels with international themes and topics. He was not very successful. Then, he began writing about what he knew. MacLennan decided to write about the Halifax explosion he survived when he was a boy. As an experiment he wrote *Barometer Rising*, which was published in 1941. His switch from international themes to Canadian ones brought him great success. It also welcomed a new phase of literature to Canada. This national focus was carried on in MacLennan's 1945 novel *Two Solitudes*. It is a story about the French-English problems in Quebec. Much of his writing was based in Montreal. However, it touched upon universal themes and ideas shared by the entire country. His novels won him the Governor General's Award three times, one of these awards being for *Two Solitudes*. He also won the award twice for his nonfiction writing. He won many other awards and became the first Canadian to receive Princeton University's James Madison Medal, which is given to a graduate who has excelled in his profession.

1947

Canada Sees the Wind

W.O. Mitchell was known for his writing about western Canada and the Prairies. His strength as a writer and his western settings influenced many other Prairie writers. In 1947, Mitchell released *Who Has Seen the Wind*, bringing him instant success and recognition. The novel explored the meanings of birth, death, life, freedom, and justice through a young boy named Brian. Mitchell captured the beauty of the Prairies and the power of the wind. The novel was translated into French in 1974 as well as several other languages. It was also made into a successful movie in 1977. W.O. Mitchell wrote several radio and television plays. Many, such as *Jake and the Kid*, originated as stories in *Maclean's* magazine and ran on CBC radio. The series was made for television in 1961, and revived in the 1990s. Some of his early plays, including *The Devil's Instrument* in 1949, were later made into full-length plays. In 1973, W.O. Mitchell became a Member of the Order of Canada.

Canada Sees the Wind

1946

The deportation of Japanese Canadian citizens after World War II becomes the subject of many books and poems.

1947

Irving Layton publishes his first collection of poetry.

1947

Published at Last

Sinclair Ross referred to *As for Me and My House*, released in 1941, as his third novel—the first two were abandoned after he could not find a publisher for them. He worked at the Royal Bank until he retired at the age of 60. He wrote books on the side. The reviews for *As for Me and My House* were glowing. The novel is a great work that explores how people feel as a result of their surroundings. The story is that of a minister and his wife. They struggle to overcome the Depression, get used to a new home in Saskatchewan, and make their relationship work. It is written as a journal. The action in the novel is presented as Mrs. Bentley, the minister's wife, sees and experiences it. Sinclair Ross also published many short stories that were well received, the most famous of which was "The Painted Door." His two novels published after *As For Me and My House* did not attract much positive attention.

Into the Future

Many books are written about significant events such as World War II and the Great Depression. Often, these books tell stories about how important events affect people's lives long after these events are no longer found in newspaper headlines. Can you think of any books that were written recently that will be a good source of history in the future?

1948
Hugh MacLennan wins the Governor General's Award.

1949
James Reaney's collction *The Red Heart* wins the Governor General's Award for Poetry.

1950
Comic book writer and illustrator John Byrne is born.

Literature
1930s

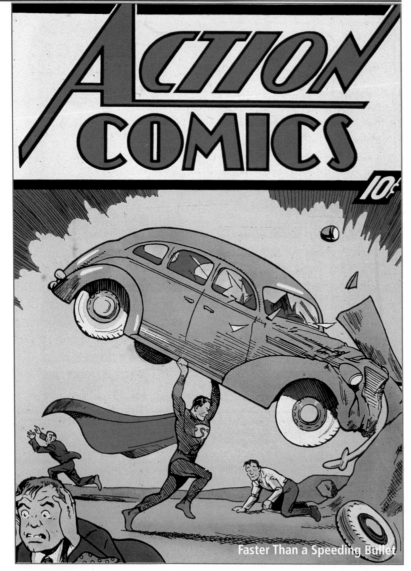

Faster Than a Speeding Bullet

someone in trouble. At first, the *Superman* comics were turned down by almost every comic publisher. Finally, Action Comics agreed to publish *Superman*. They thought that *Superman* was different enough to be successful. *Superman* was an immediate success and inspired many other comic book producers to create their own Superman-like characters. Superman was the first hero to have a secret identity and a special costume. In the first few books, Superman could leap tall buildings but could not fly. Over the years, Superman's powers increased to give readers bigger and bigger thrills.

1930s

Escape

People looked for ways to escape from hard times. Magazines provided one escape. Magazines such as *Maclean's*, *Liberty*, *Reader's Digest*, and *Life* provided romantic fictional stories that allowed readers to forget about their problems for a short while. Women's stories tended to focus on handsome, wealthy, strangers who carried the heroines away to strange, exotic places. The comings and goings of Hollywood stars also filled the pages of these monthly magazines.

1930s

Faster Than a Speeding Bullet

Superman was the brainchild of Jerry Siegel and Torontonian Joe Shuster in 1938. At first, Superman was a villain, but the two men decided he would make a better hero. The meek, mild-mannered reporter, Clark Kent, turned himself into a superhero when he heard the call of

1931
Mystery writer Howard Engel is born.

1932
Sharon Pollock, playwright for stage and radio, is born.

1933
Novelist Frederic Philip Grove publishes *Fruits of the Earth*, about prairie pioneer life.

Escape

1930s

Canadian Writers Recognized with Award

In the 1930s, Canadian writers were recognized for their hard work and accomplishments. Governor General John Buchan created the Governor General's Literary Awards to highlight the best books written in Canada each year. The first set of Governor General's Awards were presented in 1937. The award winners were chosen by the Canadian Authors Association until 1944. An independent board was then created to take over the selection of winners. The Governor General's Award remains one of the highest honours a Canadian author can receive in this country. Gwethalyn Graham won the Governor General's Award for Fiction in 1938. Bertram Brooker, Laura G. Salverson, and Franklin D. McDowell also won the award between 1936 and 1939.

Canadian Writers Recognized with Award

1934

Leonard Cohen is born.

1935

The Canadian Broadcasting Corporation forms, giving Canadian writers a chance to create their own radio plays and dramas.

SEPTEMBER 25¢

fantastic
ADVENTURES

CHILLING TALE OF AN
THE LAVEND

TRUE CRIME MYSTERIES

Formerly
FLYNN'S

Detective
NOV. 15 FICTION
Every Other Wednesday
10 cts.

The Devil's Mistress
by
RICHARD SALE

1936
The first Governor General's Awards are given to Bertram Booker for fiction and T.B. Robertson for non-fiction.

1937
Laura Salverson's *The Dark Weaver* wins the second Governor General's Award for Fiction.

Morley Callaghan

and stories from the United States did not make it to Canadian bookstore shelves.

1936

Morley Callaghan

Morley Callaghan wrote about realistic topics. His books argued that people were in control of their own lives. If they failed, they only had themselves and their choices to blame. For material, he drew on the part-time jobs he held while a student and then as an employee with a daily newspaper in Toronto. They also gave him confidence that he could write well. The 1930s was a productive period in Callaghan's career. He published seven volumes of fiction during this time, including *Such is My Beloved* and *More Joy in Heaven*. He also wrote scripts and journalism articles through the 1930s and 1940s.

1930s

Pulp Fiction

Inexpensive fiction novels were very popular. Since they were printed on cheap, brownish-paper, they were called pulp fiction—especially by people who did not approve of them. The covers often featured semi-nude women, and the titles were sensational. The book titles included *Weird Tales*, *The Bride Wore Black*, *Listen to the Madman's Drum*, and *All These Must Die*. These books made perfect reading for people who wanted to escape from their troubles. Canadian censors made sure that the more spicy covers

Into the Future

Reading has always been a popular way to relax and relieve stress. In the early 1930s, the Great Depression gave many people a reason to want to exercise their imaginations. Today, people will often read fiction or fantasy books to refresh themselves, and set aside their worries for a while. What makes you want to read?

1938
Joe Shuster and Jerry Siegal create the Superman character.

1939
Poet bill bissett is born.

1940
Stephen Leacock publishes *The British Empire*.

Children's Books

Children's Books

In the 1920s, Lucy Maud Montgomery's books about Anne of Green Gables were popular among girls. Soon, a new series called *The Hardy Boys* caught the imaginations of the boys. Leslie McFarlane was a journalist from Haileybury, Ontario. He wrote the first 21 books in the *Hardy Boys* series under the **pseudonym** Franklin W. Dixon. When McFarlane moved on, another writer continued with the series under the same name without the appearance of any change. *The Hardy Boys* is the all-time longest-running and best-selling series for boys. The books have been translated into many languages and sold worldwide. Although teachers and libraries thought the books were poor fiction in the 1920s, the books continued to be a big hit with children. Over the next several decades, *The Hardy Boys* series was made into a television series, a cartoon, stage plays, and comic books. Toys based on the series were also created.

Happy Canadian Endings

After living through the horrors of World War I, Canadians wanted to read books that had a happy ending. They wanted adventure and romance. There was a growth in nationalism in Canadian art and literature, and people began buying and reading fiction by Canadian writers. The Canadian Authors Association was founded in 1921 to promote nationalism and convince Canadians to buy Canadian rather than American books. Mazo de la Roche's stories about a Canadian family named Whiteoak, who lived in a house called Jalna, were an instant success. She wrote 16 more Jalna novels, which are full of romance and had happy endings. Books that did not follow the "happily ever after" formula were less popular. Several novels that are now highly regarded were criticized. Some were banned. They dealt with themes that were thought vulgar and not suitable for Canadian readers. In 1928, Toronto writer Morley Callaghan wrote a novel called *Strange Fugitive* about an alcohol bootlegger. The content of the story caused it to be termed an "American novel," and it did not sell well in Canada. Some people wanted it banned. Callaghan proved that so-called American books were not necessarily written by American authors.

1921
Abbé Lionel Adolphe Groulx writes the strongly patriotic *Vers L'émancipation*.

1922
Writer Mavis Gallant is born.

1923
Duncan Campbell Scott releases his second compilation of short stories.

1924

McGill University starts publishing
the *McGill Daily Literary Supplement*.

1925

Author Monica Hughes is born in
England. She later moves to Canada.

1920

Places to Write

Many newspapers and magazines carried **serialized** fiction stories. Most of the stories were written to a formula, like the Harlequin and Silhouette romances of today. The stories usually had a moral, or lesson, at the end. The Canadian magazine *Maclean's* was an especially popular publication. *Maclean's* included nonfiction articles, "how-to" articles, and fiction. It was published twice a month and sold for 15 cents in 1923. In 1925, *Maclean's* published 100 short stories, plus eight novels or novelettes by Canadian writers. Most of *Maclean's* fiction promoted romance and fantasy. Its editor told a group of Canadian authors that it would publish adventure and love stories written "in a lighter vein."

1923

A New Tarzan

Harold Foster was always very adventurous. At eight years old, he sailed a raft across Halifax harbour. When his family moved to Winnipeg, Foster hunted and fished to help feed the family. Later, he tried professional boxing and **prospecting** for gold. Finally, Foster decided to become an artist. To get to the Art Institute of Chicago, he bicycled 1,600 kilometres. After graduation, Foster joined the world of advertising. He designed posters and illustrated magazines. In 1929, he was hired to turn the book *Tarzan of the Apes* into a newspaper comic strip. More people probably read his Tarzan comic strip than had read Edgar Rice Burroughs' novel about Tarzan.

A New Tarzan

1926
Margaret Laurence is born in Neepawa, Manitoba.

1927
Mazo de la Roche begins her 16-novel series of the Whiteoak family with *Jalna*.

1928
Poet Nérée Beauchemin publishes *Patrie intime*.

The Most Canadian Book Ever

Stephen Leacock has been called one of the greatest writers of humour in the English language. His books sold well in the 1920s. For years, he wrote for hours every day starting at dawn. This left him time to sail, fish, tend his small farm, and teach at McGill University. He produced 35 volumes of humour during this time. Leacock was more than a funny man. On top of these volumes, he wrote 27 books of history, biography, criticism, economics, and political science. Some critics think his **satire** of the small Ontario town of Orillia in *Sunshine Sketches of a Little Town* is the most Canadian book ever written. He had people in stitches whenever he gave lectures. Leacock's humour poked fun at people's mistaken feelings of importance. Although Leacock tried to make fun of people in a kind way, people in Orillia would not forgive him for his comments in *Sunshine Sketches*. Now, however, Orillia calls itself "The Sunshine Town."

The Most Canadian Book Ever

Into the Future

Stories that have been around a long time, such as *Tarzan*, are known by many people. They are said to be part of the public's imagination. Often, to create new stories, writers will tell older stories in a new way. In 1999, Disney produced an animated movie that told the story of Tarzan once again. What other old stories can you think of that have been re-told in different ways?

1929

Poet Bliss William Carman dies.

1930

Stephen Leacock publishes *Economic Prosperity in the British Empire*.

Literature
1910s

Poem of Remembrance

100-Acre Imagination

1910s

100-Acre Imagination

Captain Harry Colebourn, an army veterinarian, saved a black bear cub from a hunter who had killed its mother. Colebourn was on his way to London, England, and picked the cub up at one of the train stops. He missed his Manitoba home, so he named the bear Winnipeg and took her to live with him in England. In 1915, Colebourn was called to France and could not take Winnie, as she was now called, with him. He gave his friendly bear to the London Zoo, where she was a favourite attraction. Writer A.A. Milne and his son, Christopher Robin, often visited Winnie at the zoo. The young boy loved the bear so much that Milne began writing stories about Winnie-the-Pooh, as Christopher called the animal. The stories were published and became a loved series around the world.

1910s

Poem of Remembrance

Lieutenant-Colonel John McCrae joined the army as a doctor. He witnessed the horror of the Battle of Ypres in 1915, after which he was put in charge of medicine at a hospital in Boulonge, France. Although he left the area, McCrae could not forget Ypres. He had seen his friends killed around him in the fighting. The experience affected him deeply. He wrote "In Flanders Fields," a poem about the soldiers who would not be coming home from the war. The poem appeared **anonymously** in *Punch*, an English magazine in 1915. Only after his death were McCrae's other poems released. *In Flanders Fields and Other Poems* was published in 1919, one year after McCrae's death.

1910s

Critic and Humourist

Stephen Leacock was more than the head of the political science department at McGill University. He was also an accomplished writer. Leacock's 1914 book *Arcadian Adventures with the Idle Rich* looks at life in an American city. His sharp wit and satire is sharper in this book than any other because it is not wrapped up in emotion as were his writings about Canada. Leacock wrote more than 60 books and was awarded the Governor General's Award. He is thought of as the English-speaking world's best known humorist. He had a postage stamp issued in his honour and a medal, the Leacock Medal for Humour, was created as a tribute to his talent and accomplishments.

1911

Paul Morin pens the complex, expressive work of poetry, *Paon d'émail*.

1914

W.O. Mitchell is born in Weyburn, Saskatchewan.

1912

Women Should Return Home

During the war, women went to work to keep the home front running while men were fighting overseas. When the war ended, many people wanted things to return to what they had been before—women at home and men working. Many women were not willing to leave their jobs. Canadian magazines tried to convince women that the old ways were the good ways, and that they should return to being homemakers. *Canadian Home Journal* and *Maclean's* magazine wrote article after article about women who had tried to work and have families but failed. The women in the articles discovered that happiness was found in quitting their jobs. These publications pressured women to conform to society's traditional places. Many women ignored these messages and stayed in the workforce.

Women Should Return Home

1913

Maclean's Magazine

Maclean's magazine was started by John Bayne Maclean in 1905. It was known by many different titles in its first decade of publication. It was *The Busy Man's Magazine*, *Busy Man's*, *Business*, and *The Business Magazine*. It officially came to be called *Maclean's* in 1911. The magazine was, at first, a publication for businesspeople. The pages were filled with articles from around the world. By 1914, Maclean and his editor, T.B. Costain, realized the importance of the growing sense of nationalism in Canada. It could also be made profitable. The magazine became one about Canadian men and women, Canadian government and politics, and Canadian fiction. It was a magazine for Canadians, and sold well to people who were happy to finally read about others similar to themselves.

Maclean's **Magazine**

1910s

Outdoor Writer

Ernest Thompson Seton was best known for creating a distinctly Canadian writing style in the early part of the century—he wrote realistic animal stories. His 1906 book *Two Little Savages: Being the Adventures of Two Boys Who Lived as Indians and What They Learned*, is a classic in children's literature. He then wrote several books on woodcraft, one of which became part of the *Boy Scouts of America Official Manual* in 1910. In 1911, he wrote about a trip he made to the Far North. He called it *The Arctic Prairies: A Canoe Journey of 2000 Miles in Search of the Caribou*. In the 1920s, he released a four-volume series about game animals. He was awarded the John Burroughs and Elliott Gold medals.

Outdoor Writer

1916
Louis Hémon's *Maria Chapdelaine* is published, chronicling rural life in Quebec.

1918
Journalist and naturalist Fred Bosworth is born.

1920
Pierre Berton is born in Whitehorse, Yukon.

Literature
1900s

Lucy Maud Montgomery

1900s

Janey Canuck

Emily Murphy wrote many book reviews and articles in Canadian magazines and newspapers. She took on the pen name Janey Canuck under which she published four popular books. Among her most famous books were *The Impressions of Janey Canuck Abroad* (1901), and *Janey Canuck in the West* (1910). Outside of her professional life, she took a keen interest in children's and women's rights.

1904

Montreal Poet

Emile Nelligan was a French-Canadian poet who lived his entire life in Montreal. He is considered by many critics to be the most outstanding turn-of-the-century Canadian writer. His talent was legendary, and he wrote all of his more than 170 poems between the ages of 17 and 20. In 1899, at 20 years of age, he suffered a mental breakdown and was taken to hospital where he spent the rest of his life. His work was first published in a collection in 1904.

1908

Lucy Maud Montgomery

At the turn of the 20th century, Prince Edward Island writer Lucy Maud Montgomery scribbled the following idea for a story in her notebook: "Elderly couple apply to orphan asylum for a boy. By mistake a girl is sent to them." The success of *Anne of Green Gables*, which was published in 1908, came as a complete surprise to Montgomery. More Than 80 years later, Anne Shirley is the best-known fictional character in Canadian history, and *Anne of Green Gables* has been read by more people than any other Canadian book. Hollywood has since filmed three *Anne* movies. Several related television miniseries, including *Emily of New Moon*, have been produced. Montgomery was born in 1874 in the little village of Clifton, where her father worked in the village general store. When she was 21 months old, her mother died of **tuberculosis**, and her father moved west to Saskatchewan to start a new life. Maud was sent to Cavendish, P.E.I., to be raised by her grandparents. To earn a living, Montgomery became a schoolteacher. When her grandfather died in 1898, Maud left teaching, a career she did not enjoy, and returned to Cavendish to take care of her grandmother. She also devoted time to writing. Her first novel, *Anne of Green Gables*, became an international success. After her grandmother died in 1911, Montgomery married Reverend Ewan Macdonald and moved to Ontario. There, she published another 16 novels. When Montgomery died in 1942, she was buried in Cavendish.

Montreal Poet

1902
Leslie McFarlane, first writer of the *Hardy Boys* series, is born.

1902
Poet Bliss Carman begins his 5-volume series, *The Pipes of Pan*.

1903
Morley Callaghan is born.

Robert Service

1900s

Robert Service

Robert Service was born in England in 1874 and immigrated to Canada when he was 20. He ended up in Dawson City in the Yukon and worked for the Canadian Bank of Commerce. He also wrote poetry. In 1907, his first book of poetry, called *Songs of a Sourdough*, was published. Service's poems were immediately popular. *Ballads of a Cheechako* followed in 1909 and *Rhymes of a Rolling Stone* in 1912. *The Trail of '98*, a novel, was published in 1910. Service left Canada shortly afterwards. During World War I, he served as an ambulance driver. He never lived in Canada again and died in France in 1958. His poems "The Shooting of Dan McGrew" and "The Cremation of Sam McGee" remain popular Canadian folklore to this day, and his poetry made the Canadian North come alive for many around the world.

1900s

Ralph Connor

Reverend Charles Gordon, who wrote under the pseudonym Ralph Connor, was the most successful Canadian author of the early 20th century. Some of his best-selling novels were *The Sky Pilot*, The Prospector, and *The Man From Glengarry*. Sales from his 29 books exceeded $5 million! Gordon became a minister at the age of 30. His church missions were in the West, which provided him with much of the material for his stories. His books were so popular in the United States that police had to be called to control the crowds at one of his lectures.

1900s

The Canadian Publishers

John McClelland and Frederick Goodchild founded the publishing company of McClelland and Goodchild Limited in 1906. Eight years later, George Stewart joined the company, and his name was added to the company's title. When Goodchild left the company in 1918, it became known as it is today: McClelland & Stewart Inc. At first, it was a library supply house. It then went on to become one of the most important publishing houses in Canada.

1905

Duncan Campbell Scott releases the first of his poetic collections inspired by the Ontario landscape, *New World Lyrics and Ballads*.

1908

Stephen Leacock becomes head of political science at McGill University.

Into the Future

Authors are the storytellers of the world. They entertain people, keep them informed, and help them to remember history. Some of the most famous people in history are authors, such as Homer, William Shakespeare, and J.K. Rowling. One of the best things about writing is that anyone can try it. Every author starts out with nothing more than paper, a pen, and an imagination.

Become an Author

Carry a notebook with you during the next week. Whenever you have an idea that you think is interesting, write it down in your notebook. These ideas can be pure imagination, or they could be about real things you have seen that catch your attention. At the end of the week, look at your notebook. Do any of these ideas look more interesting than the others? Pick one idea, or a few that work together, and make a story of it. The only limit is your imagination! Authors can create worlds of knights and dragons just as easily as they can write about the real world. No matter where your story is set, it needs a few important parts. All stories need a beginning, a middle, and an end. To make your story interesting, it needs a **conflict** between the characters or a problem to be solved. Writing can be difficult, but do not give up. Ask your teacher or a librarian for help if you find an idea challenging. Just like anything else, the secret to writing well is plenty of learning and practice.

FURTHER
Research

Many books and websites provide information on Canadian literature. To learn more about this topic, borrow books from the library, or surf the Internet.

Books

Most libraries have computers that connect to a database for searching for information. If you input a key word, you will be provided with a list of books in the library that contain information on that topic. Non-fiction books are arranged numerically, using their call number. Fiction books are organized alphabetically by the author's last name.

Websites

To learn more about Canadian literature, visit **www.canlit.ca**.

For additional information about Canadian literature, surf to **www.umanitoba.ca/canlit/about.shtml**.

Glossary

anonymously: publishing a piece of work without making the creator's name known

autobiography: a book that a person writes about his or her own life

balladeer: one who creates poems or songs that tell a story

conflict: a disagreement that is serious and prolonged

defector: a person who leaves his or her country to live in another one

nonfiction: a book that is based on facts rather than made-up stories

prejudiced: exhibiting an opinion or judgment based on usually negative considerations

prospecting: to search for gold or other minerals

pseudonym: a name used by an author instead of his or her own

quintessential: representing the best or most typical example of a particular style or idea

satire: use of irony to show problems of a situation; often biting

serialized: a story that is presented one part at a time

tuberculosis: an infectious disease that may affect almost any tissue in the body

Index